6 Figures in 60 Days

Welcome to the most-requested section of the entire guide. We have lots of great chapters available, such as, "Discover Your Path in Data" and "Top Questions from Real Interviews", but this is where the rubber meets the road. This is where you'll get the tools and strategy to get your dream job. This is where you'll win big.

Keep this in mind: while this is the most sought-after strategy we share, it's also the one that requires the most work from you. Getting a good job of any kind is difficult, and often data-related careers are the most competitive roles out there- what that means is that you're going to have to put in the time and effort to see yourself through to success. We're going to give you the strategy and tools you need, but we can't make you put in the work. As Jim Rohn once said, "You can't hire someone else to do your pushups for you".

Before we begin, I want to let you know that you're already succeeding. Most of the developed world looks like this: go to school, get a job you don't really like, put in an average amount of effort, maybe get a 1% raise per year (if you're lucky), and focus on your favorite television shows. That's perfectly fine for some people, but you're one of the few individuals that actually strives to better themselves. You're one of the few people that will invest both time and money into a strategy like this, and you're actually going to take action. This is a big deal, and you should be proud of yourself. My hat's off to you.

I also want to share that I think we're kindred souls. Both I and everyone else at Learn-Data was once in a situation you may be familiar with: in a job you don't like, with a little-known college brand, and no big successes in the family to learn from. We've also had to make our own way in this world. We know what it's like to stay up late working, only to get up at 4am the next morning and get back to work on the dream. We know what it's like to sacrifice free time for the dream.

Let's get down to the nitty-gritty. As I mentioned, this will work if you do. Don't start unless you're committed to seeing this through, because there will probably be times in your job search when you'll want to give up. Get committed.

We're also going to assume that you're at least somewhat qualified for a role in data. You've probably done an online course or two, or may even have a background in something quantitative. You don't have to have a long history in Data Science or Data Analytics or anything else, but if you're brand-spanking new and have never opened Excel or have no idea what SQL is, this may not be the section for you. In this case we suggest starting with the section, "Finding Your Path in Data", and then move on to "Self Taught vs. Online Courses: The Ultimate Guide". From there, we recommend getting to work teaching yourself core concepts or enrolling in an online class. You do need to have the ability to perform well in a data-driven role, and we don't want to assume that any employer is willing to train you up from zero.

That said, let's get down to business. This is going to be a fantastic section, and both your financial and time commitment will pay off exponentially. Our outcome here is to help you get a great job in data- it could be a Data Analyst, Data Scientist, Data Engineer, or any other subtypes within these roles. The structure of this section is an 8 week strategy, but keep in mind that your mileage may vary. Some people take longer to find a job, others do so much quicker. We recommend reading this section all the way through first, then going back and taking it week-by-week. That way, if you start moving quickly and have an onsite interview in week two, for example, you'll know exactly where to find the onsite preparation info in this chapter.

Are you ready? Let's do it.

One of the main themes in this chapter is going to be outreach, which to us means reaching out to connections and applying to jobs. This is a crucial part of the process, and we're going to be a little more strategic than most people are. Most potential candidates use the "spray & pray" technique: they just blast their resume out to a few role postings and then hope and pray they get an interview. Instead, we're going to be smart in our approach.

Keep this in mind: you want to keep generating opportunities, even when you get interviews. One of the biggest mistakes people make is that they stop applying for job once they've got an interview with the hiring manager or an onsite. Don't do this! You want to continue applying to jobs until the moment you've signed an offer letter. This will give you options and help free your mind from any nervousness or anxiety.

The first step: make a list of companies and roles. Use Google Sheets or something similar to create a home base listing companies, their industry, links to the role you're interested in, and fields for things like the date you applied, whether or not you were rejected, etc. This is where you're going to track everything.

Company	Industry	Personal Rank	Employee Count	Role Link 1	Role Link 2	Connection	Notes	Applied Date	Status

Ready for something outside the norm? One of our key strategies is to start applying and interviewing at the companies you're least excited about. It may sound counterintuitive, but there is great power in this. The best way to do this is to rank every company on your list from most ideal to least (1 through 100, or through however many you have), and then start applying from the **bottom** of your list.

Why do this? Wouldn't it make more sense to concentrate our efforts on the most interesting and exciting opportunities? Actually, no, and here's why: you need to practice interviewing. Let me repeat that: you need practice. It doesn't matter if you have a PhD or can write amazing machine learning code- you're going to need to get some reps under your belt in order to eventually succeed and get an offer.

This is a secret to applying to jobs that the vast majority of people don't get. Here's what most people do: they find a few jobs they'd love ("dream jobs"), get really excited, work their butt off to get an interview, and then totally mess up when they get the chance to speak with someone. They miss their opportunity at their dream role, not because they're unqualified, but because they haven't taken the time to cultivate the skill of interviewing.

If you've done this before, don't worry- everyone has. Now you know better. Now you have a strategy in play that will allow you to get exposure to multiple opportunities, sharpen your skills, and eventually get your ideal role at a fantastic company. That sounds a lot better than going for your dream role right away and blowing it.

Here's another thing you may not have thought of: go ahead and apply to roles even if you're not 100% confident you would take the role. Going through these low-risk opportunities will be a great way to sharpen your interviewing skills and get to a place where you can really perform when it's for a role you're very serious about.

"But won't I be wasting other people's time?"

Because you're a polite person, you may be concerned that applying for a job you don't really want will be dishonest or a waste of the company's time. It's good to be empathetic in this way, and you don't want to apply to jobs that you'd never take, but think about it this way- for a given role, even if you're not super interested, is there anything that would make you take the job? What if they offered you a salary of $200,000/yr? What if the manager was your ideal leader? What if the company was experiencing incredible growth and there was a clear path to a leadership role in a year or two?

Another main theme is practice. Once you do get interviews, you're going to need to take time to rehearse your answers to questions- not just writing them, but saying them out loud. This will help you become confident and ready to succeed in the interviews. You need to approach interviewing in the same way you'd approach learning SQL, Python, or any other technical skill- as a skill unto itself. Some people feel that if they have the right technical skills and meet the job requirements, they'll get the job once they get an interview. They often don't. When they don't, they usually do one of two things: blame the company or process, saying things like, "I guess they just wanted someone who went to Harvard" (or something similar), or they feel that their coding or technical skills were the reason they didn't receive the opportunity, so they enroll in another online course, put in the work, and get the credential- only to find themselves in the same position later.

Let's be clear: the opportunities you receive are a function of your value (ability to do the job, potential, etc.), and your ability to communicate that value. You get what you communicate. Write that down now- you get what you communicate!

Week 1

Alright, week one is where it all gets started. If you haven't made your list of companies yet, go ahead and re-read the section above and create the spreadsheet. This is going to allow you to keep lots of opportunities going at the same time, track your progress, and identify your weak points so you know exactly what to improve.

Once you've got that, it's time to get started. Your first step is to stack-rank your list, with #1 being the job you want most and the last number being the job you're least interested in. When your list is ranked, sort it from high to low- we're going to start with the least-desirable opportunities on your list. Let's review the why behind this one more time: starting with the least-desirable companies will help you get practice without risking losing out on something fantastic. Consider this free 1:1 tutoring in interview skills, or at least as close as you can get without paying someone huge sums of money. Remember, you're not doing anything wrong by taking this approach as long as you're open to the possibility of working with these companies. Who knows? Maybe you'll be surprised by one of these "not-as-good" opportunities and go ahead and take it. Some readers have interviewed at a company they didn't think was very interesting, but found out there was a great growth strategy and they really clicked with the hiring manager- and they ultimately took the job over their "top companies".

Now what? The next step can be somewhat daunting if you don't have much experience: outreach. Outreach, for our purposes, simply means applying to jobs directly (reaching out to the company) or reaching out to connections in your network that may be able to help you get an interview. We're going to go over the latter in detail, but first let's make sure we understand how to apply directly online correctly.

Applying Online

Is it true that all online job postings are simply a, "black hole" for resumes? Not at all. Companies large and small actively review applications that come through online and move candidates to the interview stage if they think there's a potential fit. You're probably going to apply to many jobs through online portals, so there are a few things to keep in mind:

Make sure your resume looks great and speaks to the job you're applying for. For now just make sure it's one page (seriously), highlights your relevant accomplishments, and doesn't have a ton of fluff that is irrelevant to the job. Did you get a silver medal for a marketing competition in college five years ago? Go ahead and leave it out unless you're applying for a marketing role. Last piece of advice: don't obsess over the resume. Find some good examples online, copy them, and move on.

You won't hear back on a lot of applications- don't read into it too much. It's highly unlikely that you're going to get an interview for every application, so when you get a rejection letter (or nothing at all), just keep your head up and keep moving. The other side to this is that if you're submitting a lot of applications (in the ballpark of 20) and you're getting rejected for everything, you may need to re-think the roles you're applying to. Are they entry-level, or do they require a lot of experience you don't have? If you're not getting any interviews at all it may be time to apply to a different type of role, potentially something with slightly lower requirements.

These are the basics of submitting job applications online. Don't expect miracles, but plenty of people get great jobs starting with an online application process. Still, we want to make sure we're being as effective as possible, and applying through a referral is one of the best ways to put yourself in the running for a great job. Let's take a look at how that works.

Our basic process here is that, for companies on our list, we're going to leverage a social network (LinkedIn is the best for this) to find connections that work at the company, or connections of connections that work at the company. One basic way to do this is to just use LinkedIn search tools to look up employees in the company who are a 1st or 2nd connection.

Let's say you found an interesting role at Google. Start by looking for connections you have that work at Google (meaning you and the person are directly connected). If you can find someone, shoot them a message that says something like:

"Hi Sam,

Hope you're doing well. I'm reaching out because I saw an interesting Product Analyst role open at Google that looks like it fits my experience pretty well. Would you be open to submitting a referral for me?

Thanks,

Your Name"

That's it- short and sweet. Don't write a lot and don't complicate it. They don't need to know excessive details about the bootcamp you went to or about how this is your dream job. Write a greeting, tell them why you're reaching out, and ask them one simple yes or no question. Nothing more. It's highly likely that they'll say, "Sure, can you send me your resume and a link to the role?" Then you're set.

You can also do this for 2nd level connections (people who are connected to somebody you're connected to, but not connected directly to you). This will be a little different because you're not going to reach out to the person at the company directly- you're going to reach out to the person you know. Here's what it looks like: let's say you're interested in an Operations Analyst role at Uber. You look through LinkedIn to see if you're connected to anyone at Uber, but no luck. You do see that your friend Tom is connected to someone named Kara who works in recruiting at Uber. Here's what you send:

"Hi Tom,

Hope you're doing well. I'm reaching out because I've been looking into some roles at Uber, and I noticed you're connected to Kara ___. Do you know her well enough to introduce me? (Include a link to the person's profile)

Thanks,

Your Name"

	Short and sweet. Sensing a theme here? Give them a greeting, tell them why you're reaching out, and ask a simple yes or no question. If they do connect that person, use the other email template above (mention the exact position) and ask for a referral. This is the formula for successful outreach, and it's not complicated.

	To sum it up, our three buckets for outreach are direct applications, reaching out to connections that work at the company, and reaching out to connections who are connected to people that work at the company. Your chances at landing an interview will be better with referrals, but you can still get interviews for great jobs by applying online.

	The main thing here is to stay on top of outreach throughout the process and keep lots of opportunities on your plate. One of the biggest mistakes candidates make is spending all their time and effort on one or two companies, then having to start from scratch after a few weeks. We want to have lots of options so we're constantly moving in the right direction.

	Lastly, here are a few reminders: make sure you start with the least-desirable companies first. This will enable you to get plenty of practice having conversations, and by the time you get to the big leagues you'll be polished and ready.

You also want to make sure you're taking good notes and tracking your progress. Create a spreadsheet with companies, roles, dates you applied, when the recruiter reached out, and what the status is (applied, rejected, interviewing, offer). On the same spreadsheet, create another tab that will serve as a repository for all the questions you're asked during the process. While you're on the phone with recruiters, make a note of the questions they asked (as long as it doesn't interfere with your concentration). Pro tip: make sure you use pen and paper, rather than typing on the computer- the person on the other end of the phone can hear you typing, and it's annoying and slightly odd.

Whether you take notes during the call or not, do a quick post-mortem after each call. In the spreadsheet, write each question asked, who asked it (e.g. recruiter, hiring manager), what your response was, and what you'd do better next time. As you accumulate questions, you'll start to notice the same questions asked over and over- that means you should spend time writing out your answers and practicing them out loud.

While you're evaluating the call, it's also a good idea to note anything the recruiter mentioned that may be valuable to you later. For example, a recruiter might say, "Yea, believing in our mission is something they look for". Great! Now you know that when you have a call with the hiring manager you'll want to be able to articulate how the company's mission resonates with you personally. The best candidates understand this: recruiters are your friend. They want you to succeed. They are trying to fill roles and their performance is often judged based on how many candidates they bring in that are ultimately hired. It doesn't mean you can be bad or sloppy- it just means that you both want the same thing- to get a great job and be successful.

Week 2

By Week 2, you should have a good groove going. You've probably got a routine of reaching to people or applying to 3-5 jobs per day, and what's important at this point is to stick to it. One way that people go wrong is that they reach out to lots of people, send out lots of applications, and finally start getting interviews, and when they do, they stop applying to jobs. Don't do that! Even as you get interviews, keep reaching out to connections and applying to jobs- you want to have a lot of opportunities on your plate. Keep creating new opportunities for yourself until you have a signed offer, period.

Outreach in this stage shouldn't be any different than last week, so we won't spend a ton of time on it. Hopefully you're getting some recruiter interviews set up, so we're going to focus on doing a great job when you actually get on the phone with someone. The preparation process is fairly straightforward, but there are a few dos and don'ts.

Do:
Understand what the company does at a basic level
Get a list of questions (we have a list in this section)
Physically write your answers down
Practice your answers out loud

Don't:
Look up company-specific questions on Glassdoor or online
Spend a disproportionate amount of time on any one interview
Get too stressed or nervous

When it comes to the questions themselves, candidates often want to dive deep into Glassdoor or scour Google for exact interview questions a particular company will ask. If they're interviewing at Twitter, they want to know what the questions are for Twitter. If they're interviewing at Airbnb, they want to know exactly what Airbnb asks. Here's the thing: recruiters almost always ask the same questions, regardless of whether it's a huge tech company or a small startup.

Recruiters want to know:
- About your current role and how well your experience fits the role they have open
- Why you're interested in the company
- Basic items like compensation expectations, verifying you're willing to work where the role is located, etc.

That's mostly it. You might get some questions like, "What tech stack do you use?" or "What's your familiarity with SQL?", but the good news is that you can study and practice the same 10 or so questions for recruiter calls and you'll generally be set for any company you apply to. The main message here is that you shouldn't spend a lot of your time researching specific interview questions for recruiter calls. That time is better spent writing out your answers and practicing saying them out loud. Our other chapter, "Top Questions from Real Interviews", will have specific interview questions, but for now keep these themes in mind.

Lastly, it's natural to feel a little anxious about interviews, but don't get too stressed or nervous. The strategy we're laying out here is exactly what will help curb that anxiety and help you be relaxed and performing really well. You're going to get lots of practice repetitions at the "Tier 2" companies before you go after the big ones. Every time you do an interview, you get more comfortable (so do lots of them). You're also going to be very prepared for the interviews you do have. Writing interview answers down and practicing them out loud will be a tremendous boost to your confidence, which by itself will help you communicate clearly and with passion, and you'll have much more success.

At the end of the day, just enjoy these conversations and learn what you can. You're going to have lots of opportunities in your career, and no one job is going to make or break your life. If you're the type of person who has invested in this program and is willing to put in the effort, things are going to work out well for you over time.

Week 3

Wow, three weeks already- time is probably flying by for you, and that's a good thing. At this point you may be getting interviews with hiring managers. If not, don't worry- just keep doing outreach and use the info in the Week 2 section to do a great job on recruiter calls.

In this section we're going to discuss the hiring manager interview, which usually comes after the recruiter interview, as well as the data challenge. The purpose of the recruiter interview is to make sure you meet the base qualifications for the role, and the hiring manager is going to take that one step further to understand your abilities at a deeper level and get a sense of how you'd fit into the team's mission.

These interviews can vary a bit, but they often involve the hiring manager telling you about the role and team, you explaining your experience, and a case question. A "case" question is essentially a mock scenario that is a good example of what the role will entail. Here's an example question that a company like Uber might ask:

"Let's say that the number of new drivers goes down. How would you dig into that metric to figure out what the problem is?"

As you can see, it's more about getting an idea of your thought process than it is determining whether or not you know a specific technical concept.

These questions are very important. It's often the case that hiring managers want to know that you have a strong problem-solving ability and coherent thought process more than they want someone to have experience in some particular statistical theory or something of that nature. This is your chance to shine and show that you're a logical and creative thinker that can solve problems effectively.

How do you find and practice these problems? This is the time to look up questions specific to the company. If you're interviewing for a Data Scientist role at Uber, start Googling Data Scientist interview questions at Uber. For the big companies you should be able to find some good information, but if you're interviewing at a smaller company or just aren't finding questions, try looking up a competitor or getting more general in your search. "Data Analyst Interview Questions" or "Data Scientist Interview Questions" should have some good results.

One more thing to keep in mind: make sure that you're writing down the questions you're asked as much as you can, as well as your answers. At the end of the week, evaluate yourself and write out how you could have answered the question better. Over time this information will be a treasure-trove of valuable insight into the typical questions for the role you're targeting. Also be sure to keep your tracker up to date (applied, interviewing, rejected, etc.). The tracker should be completed in such a way that anyone can glance at it and within 60 seconds understand what you've done and where you are in your job search.

Now, let's discuss the infamous data challenge.

If you've made it this far, you're doing incredibly well- congratulations! The data challenge is a way for a company to understand your ability to think through problems and present analyses in a compelling way. These are typically larger, multi-part prompts that ask you to analyze a data set, dig into abnormalities and/or find opportunities, discuss your findings, and recommend action items. They are most common for Analyst and Data Scientist paths, but are possible for other data roles as well.

The first step is that the recruiter will let you know how much time you'll have to complete the data challenge (usually 2-4 days), and will ask when you'd like to receive it. Always schedule it so you'll have a full weekend to work on the project. For example, if the assignment needs to be returned in 48hrs, ask to have it sent early Saturday morning (recruiters can schedule these emails, so they don't have to send it to you manually). You're going to want to give yourself a full two days to work on it if needed.

When the time comes, the recruiter will email you a prompt and a dataset, usually in CSV form, although occasionally a company will you have pull data from a cloud database such as BigQuery. He or she will also remind you of the timeline for delivery. The prompt will have the details of the challenge, and will also say something like, "The estimated time to complete this is 3-5hrs". Ignore this. You should absolutely take as much time as you need. There are no extra points for doing it within the "estimated time", and It's incredibly rare that anyone from the company would ask how long you spent on the data challenge. If they do, just be honest and say you got really interested in the project and time flew by.

Your first priority is to not be overwhelmed, worried, or stressed. When you get the email, don't start reading the prompt until you're actually ready to get started and spend at least an hour working on it. For example, if you're going to grab coffee with a friend Saturday morning, don't read the prompt and then walk out the door to meet up with them. This is for two reasons: 1. Some people get stressed, and it affects their mental state negatively, and 2. Even if you don't get stressed, your brain might start to come up with hypotheses and explanations for whatever problem you're going to work on, without even having looked at the data! You don't want to approach the data with mental biases because they can prevent you from seeing the truth in the data.

When you do settle in to work on it, get excited. This is an excellent way to show your skills, and for most people it's a lot better than an extra 2-3hrs of technical and problem solving in-person interviews. In the comfort of your own home you'll be able to relax and enjoy the process of solving interesting problems with data. One note: a data challenge is almost always reflective of the work you'd be performing on the job, so if for some reason it's something you would never have an interest in doing, you may want to bow out of the process. This is unlikely if you've made it this far, but keep in mind that it will line up pretty closely with your day-to-day.

Once you are settled in, read the prompt fully. One of the biggest mistakes candidates make is that they read the first question and jump right in. DON'T TOUCH THE DATA YET! You need to develop a firm understanding of the entire problem and how the questions are connected before you start writing code. Read the prompt fully.

The next step is to start taking notes. Copy the prompt into a Gdoc or your preferred text editor (or print it out and take notes by hand). At this point you also want to look at the datasets and see what you're working with. You should be able to answer each one of these questions:

What is Question 1 asking me? How would I restate it in my own words? What about Question 2… etc.?

What is the general theme I'm sensing from the questions? What business problem am I solving? Am I digging into a metric anomaly? Am I looking for ways to increase users, revenue, etc.?

What's being asked of me? Am I being asked to come up with new product features? Am I being asked to recommend a strategy? Will I be presenting this to a group in my onsite?

Who is the audience? Am I presenting this to the Head of Data Science, or the Head of Marketing, or both? Hint: most data challenges have an audience of multiple stakeholders, including technical and non-technical.

What's my output? Is it slides? Is it a written document? Is it up to me? Pro tip: if the prompt leaves the presentation medium up to you, use slides (Google Slides is pretty good). Everyone makes fun of PowerPoint and slides in general, but it's a medium that makes it easy to communicate and get your point across, and it's something that most people are used to receiving on a daily basis. Use slides unless the prompt asks you for another format or specifically asks that you not use slides.

Again, don't write one word of code until you're able to answer the above questions. Preparation is crucial in data challenges, and is also one of the things separating really effective people from novices in a real-life work setting.

Your preparation phase should take anywhere from 20 minutes to 1 hour. Creating a plan is going to not only help you execute the task more effectively, but will also give you confidence and help you feel in command of the situation. This is a lot different than what happens to most candidates, which is that they jump in with both feet, start writing lots of code, have to backtrack and effectively waste several hours of time, and ultimately feel stressed, overwhelmed, and desperate. Preparing as prescribed will help you win in the end, so follow this plan and you'll be in great shape.

Once you've got a good idea of what the prompt is asking and what your approach will be, start doing your exploratory data analysis. We won't go into too much detail here because there is a lot of variability depending on the prompt, dataset, and role you're applying for, but use the skills you've developed in your online learning or self-study to work through the challenge effectively. If it's difficult, that's good- it's supposed to be a challenge.

Once you've worked through the problem, developed some hypotheses, and feel like you have a good point of view, you need to create the deliverable. We'll assume you're going to create a short presentation (slides).

First of all, go back and check the prompt to see if they gave you direction on the number of slides, and plan to follow it if so. If they say, "Your presentation should be 8-10 slides", make it 10 slides. Not 11. Most companies will impose a limit on slide count because A. they don't want to spend tons of time reading your presentation, and B., it forces you to be clear and concise with your findings. In the real world you're not going to be able to do 50 slides for a small or medium-sized project because no one would want to sit through that.

The data challenge is great for testing your ability to work through problems and write code, but what most people don't realize is that the company is also testing for your ability to communicate. "Right" or "wrong" isn't as important as your ability to take a vague problem, form logical and coherent ideas based on data, and communicate those ideas.

Just like communication is important in your interviews, it's important here. The people who succeed at the highest level aren't necessarily the greatest technologists in the world (although they can be), but they are the people who can communicate the best. Think about Elon Musk. He is certainly a genius, but is he the most knowledgeable person in the world about electric cars? Nope. Is he the greatest rocket engineer on the planet? Not even close. He succeeds because he does understand things at a technical level, and he's able to articulate a vision that people find compelling. Cheap space travel. Saving the planet by reducing emissions. These are large, audacious goals that anyone can understand and rally behind, and that's why people are willing to not only invest in him, but follow him.

The great news is that this is within your power- you just have to apply yourself. Communicate clearly. Start with a few bullet-point summary of your ideas, and then show the audience how you came to those conclusions. Avoid text-heavy slides and use charts and visuals when you can. Give a simple recommendation or set of recommendations that anyone can interpret easily. If you can, quantify the upside of going forward with your recommendation(s) and acknowledge the downside. Be thoughtful in your approach and you will do well.

That's about it. The data challenge is often a lot of work, but it's also often the most enjoyable part of the process. Many candidates find that they love doing the project and are excited to the same kind of work in the role, which is a fantastic situation to be in.

When it's finally done, save the documents (usually as a PDF) and send to the recruiter. Feel free to add a note letting them know you enjoyed working on the project (you can even say it was, "fun"). Then you can relax and move on to other things. Expect to wait up to a week to hear back, and it's probably OK to follow-up at around the 3-day mark unless the recruiter said it would take longer.

Week 4

Alright, so now you've been searching for jobs for one month. If you don't have an offer by now, don't worry- it's perfectly normal. It can take several weeks to several months to get an offer for a role, depending on your level of outreach, what roles you're going for, the time of year, and the job market where you live.

Realistically it doesn't matter how long it takes, does it? If you had a baby, how long would you give him to walk before you said, "OK, that's enough. I guess you're not going to walk." Every parent in the world would have their child keep trying until they figured it out- that's why most people in the world walk.

You need a similar mentality in your job search, but we'll refine it a little bit. If this is something you really want to do, you're going to keep trying until you get the result you're after. Our key to success is that we're going to be constantly improving and learning from every mistake and failure. Every time you have an interview, you're going to get better. Every time you do a data challenge, you're going to get better. Every single time.

A few strategic notes: as always, keep track of questions and do weekly post-mortems on what you can improve. Getting a job is a skill, and you need to constantly improve that skill. Secondly, don't be afraid to change course a little bit. One thing I see with some candidates is that they aim super high and lose sight of what's realistic for them at this point in their career. For example, if you took a 6-week course in data science and have a Bachelor's degree in communications, it's not likely you're going to get an offer for Senior Machine Learning Engineer role at Google right now. To be clear, you can have anything you want over time, provided you put in the work and develop yourself. Just know that for certain positions it may take some time to build up to be ready to enter that role.

Another example: let's say you want to be a Data Scientist, but after 50 applications you haven't had one hiring manager interview. You could keep trying, or you could explore Data Analyst roles at companies that have a strong Data Science team. While being a Data Analyst isn't your ultimate outcome, it could be a great way to get your foot in the door at a great company. From there you can prove yourself and eventually work your way into a Data Scientist role. Know this: for people with non-traditional backgrounds, it is much easier to move to a more advanced position within a company (by doing great work, building relationships, etc.) than it is to get an advanced position at a brand new company. Assuming you have good relationships and do great work, your current company is much more likely to take a chance on you than an outside company will be. The moral of the story is: aim high, but don't be afraid to adjust along the way and consider potential "stepping-stone" jobs that will help you reach your ultimate destination.

Week 5-7

Somewhere in weeks 5-7 you'll probably have onsite interviews. If this hasn't happened for you yet, don't worry- just stay on top of the process outlined in early weeks: maintain a good level of outreach, focus on the right things at the right time, and learn from every interaction/interview you have. Keep going and eventually you will get where you want to go.

One small note- if you've been actively reaching out about 10-20 jobs per week for five weeks, and haven't made it to the hiring manager interview yet, it may be time to step back and think about how "near-term realistic" you're being. As we said in the previous section, you can eventually do any role you want, no matter how sophisticated it sounds. You could even be a brain surgeon if you wanted to. That said, things don't always work with the timeline you have in mind. To be as extreme as possible and continue with the brain surgeon analogy: yes, you can definitely become a brain surgeon, but you won't become one with just a bachelor's degree, no matter how interested and passionate you are. You'd need to go through the process of getting your doctorate, doing a medical residency, etc., and then you'd get to operate on people's brains.

Thankfully no job in data is like brain surgery, and the vast majority aren't life and death. The education requirements that are a big barrier in fields such as medicine aren't as much as a barrier for us. What is important, however, is experience. Even roles that say they require a Master's or PhD in the job description will have exceptions for people who have "equivalent practical experience", which is great for those that are self-taught.

What we're driving at here is that there is a certain point in which it may make sense to temporarily lower your sights in order to eventually get your dream job, or what you think is your dream job. As we said in the previous section, there are a lot of great "stepping stone" jobs, such as a Data Analyst, that can lead to some of the more desired roles such as Data Scientist or Data Engineer. Be smart and think about how to best get to your ultimate outcome strategically, rather than getting fixated on one specific job title.

Let's get back to the meat of this chapter: onsite interviews. These are the most exciting part of the job hunt, but also the most daunting. First of all, if you've got an onsite interview, you should absolutely be happy and proud of yourself for getting this far. Onsites can range from a few hours to a full day, and no company would ever waste this time on someone who couldn't do the role- this means that when a company brings you onsite they are serious about hiring you. Congratulations!

The work isn't over yet, though. For a single role, companies are probably bringing 3-6 candidates in to the office for interviews, and you have to be the best one. The good news is that you can practice hard and smart, and take advantage of all the controllables to give yourself a great chance of succeeding. Let's get started.

The process will start with scheduling, and once the date is confirmed the recruiter will give you a list of people you'll be interviewing with. Pay attention to this, because we're going to do research on these people later. Some companies will also tell you what type of interview each person (or group of people) will be conducting: technical, culture fit, business case, etc. That is very valuable information to understand.

Our first step is to look back at the role posting (you kept the link in your doc, right?). Create a doc in Google Docs or wherever you take notes, and start by pasting in the job description and requirements. Now, you're going to go through the job description line-by-line, picking out pieces of information and taking notes on the work you've done that is applicable to the specific point. For example, let's say you're interviewing for a Data Scientist role, and one of the bullet points in the job description is this:

"Utilize statistical or machine learning techniques to assess marketing efficiency and recommend optimal spend by channel and by product"

Underneath that line in your doc, write down anything and everything you can think of that relates to this, even if it was just a project you did in your spare time. If there's a bullet point where you literally have no experience, just make a note and move on to the next item (we'll circle back to that later).

This is an extremely important step, so don't skip it! Hiring managers/companies aren't just interested in your skills- they're interested in your applicable skills. Throughout the interview process they'll be asking themselves, "Will this person be happy and successful in this role specifically?". By understanding this and implementing this strategy you're able to give yourself a leg up on the competition. You want to brainstorm all the work you've done related to the exact job you're interviewing for, and tailor your communication to speak to that specifically.

Here's one way that people trip themselves up: they emphasize the "cool" projects they've done, or work that they find interesting, rather than focusing on what the hiring manager is interested in (which you know from the job description). Neural nets are really cool, but if it's not a part of the job description and wouldn't realistically come in to play in the role, don't bring it up! It sounds very counterintuitive, but companies are more interested in finding a great fit for the exact position than they are interested in someone who's done a lot of cool projects.

As you can see, it is crucial that you fit in to what the hiring manager is looking for specifically. It's good to let yourself shine- just know that their main concern is bringing on someone who will be happy and successful in the role, rather than someone who is good at lots of different things and may be more interested in different types of work.

Our next step is research. We can chunk this into a few categories: research on the company itself, research on the people you're interviewing with, and research on the questions you'll be asked. With those in mind, let's dive in.

First, you want to start digging into the company itself, starting with some high-level information: What do they do? How do they monetize their business? In what ways are they expanding? We can use a company like Lyft to illustrate. If you've got an onsite with Lyft you definitely know that their in the ride-hailing business and compete with Uber. What else could you find if you started digging in? You might use Google or ask around and find out that they're interested in expanding the business-to-business part of their revenue, which could potentially be selling Lyft credit packages to companies as a perk for their employees. You may also come across info that you didn't realize: for example, did you know that (as of the time of this writing), Lyft operates predominantly in the US, with just a little penetration in Canada but no where else in the world? Unless you found that information out, you might have guessed that such a big company offered their service all over the world, particularly since their main competitor (Uber) operates in lots of international markets.

You could use that information in a few different ways. First of all, being informed about the business helps you know what not to bring up. In the case of Lyft, when you're asked about what you're looking for in your next role, you'll want to leave out anything like, "Working for a company with a big international reach". It sounds obvious, but you'd be surprised what candidates say in interviews!

You can also use the information to craft your own thought-provoking questions. For example, in your Lyft interview you might ask, "What does international expansion look like for Lyft over the next 3-5 years?" This is a great question because you get to learn about the strategic direction of the company and position yourself as someone who's interested in the long-term vision.

Make sure that you devote a good amount of time to researching the company, how they operate, how they're expanding, and their values. It is very important to get an understanding of the company's values and think about how you relate to them. For example, one of Google's core values is: "Focus on the user and all else will follow". Prior to the interview you'd want to think about this and the other values, and think about your viewpoint. In this case, when have you "focused on the user"? Why do you think that is important? Having a great understanding of the company's values will help you succeed in the interview. In fact, many companies have a "culture interview" as a part of the onsite process to make sure that whichever candidate they hire will fit in with the values of the company.

Our main strategy during the research phase is to look up themes and ideas, and start making lists of potential questions. You should also leverage sites like Glassdoor and Blind, as well as general Google searching, to find actual questions asked in interviews. Amass a list of questions, then trim the list by combining questions that are roughly the same. For example, if you have one question that asks you to dig into a decline in a delivery orders metric, and another that asks you to investigate a large spike in new user traffic, you can safely combine them because the general methodology will be the same.

The point here isn't to memorize answers to specific questions- it's to gain an understanding of the types of questions you're likely to be asked and then create a framework for answering them effectively. Your total list of questions, including technical questions, shouldn't be longer than 20-30 questions.

Next step: write answers down and practice saying them out loud. This is one of the most valuable things you'll do in your job search. Make sure that your answers are clear, concise, and correct. Make sure they address the question without being too wordy. Do research and see if you can find other perspectives on the same questions. Being thoughtful and putting in the effort at this stage will help increase your chances of success in the interview and will keep you on the path to getting your dream job.

Once you've got your confidence up for the interview, it's time to research your interviewers. The recruiter should let you know ahead of time whom you'll be interviewing with, so grab that list and start looking people up on LinkedIn (if the recruiter hasn't sent you that list, go ahead and ask). You don't have to go crazy and memorize the interviewers' life stories, and it's probably a bit too much to look them up on Facebook or Instagram. At this point, our goal is to find out a little bit about the interviewers' backgrounds, but more importantly we want to understand what roles they're in so we can better anticipate the type of conversation we'll be having.

Here's some basic info on what various roles might be interested in knowing when you interview with them, but keep in mind that these are just some patterns we've seen in candidate interviews, and not necessarily set in stone. The hiring manager will typically want to know how you'll fit into the team, and may ask case-type questions to get a sense of your problem-solving ability. Candidates often say that these interviews aren't the most difficult ones and tend to be more casual and conversational. Some hiring managers will even say something like, "I'm glad you're here and I'm excited for you to meet everyone. I don't have a lot of questions planned but I'd love to chat and answer any questions you have." All of that said, make sure you bring your A-game. Hiring decisions don't come down to a vote- the hiring manager will be the one who ultimately decides to extend an offer or not. Smile, be friendly, and be prepared to answer case questions as well as questions about why you're interested in joining, what you think about the industry the company is in, etc. If you're interviewing at Apple, talk about how the mission resonates with you and how you're excited about the future of the company. The hiring manager wants to know that you're a great fit and you'll be excited to work at the company.

In addition to the hiring manager, data role onsites often have you meet with a current member of the team or someone who would essentially be a peer of yours. Usually these interviews are going to focus on your technical skills, potentially some case-style questions, and your ability to collaborate effectively. Teammates and peers want to know that you can do the job you're interviewing for, so make sure to brush up on your technical skills and your ability to work through case questions. One note- the recruiter will almost always let you know which interview is the technical interview, but they probably won't have any information about what exactly will be covered. Go back to the job description and read it carefully- what technical skills do they mention? For most data-oriented jobs, SQL is a must, and Python is a big plus (sometimes required for more advanced roles). Also, make sure to give your resume a once-over and be prepared to answer questions based on anything you've listed (anything on your resume is fair game). SQL and Python are typical, but some interviewers will even pull out Tableau if you've got it on your resume- don't be the person that can't do what they said on their resume.

It's highly likely you'll also have interviews with people on other teams, often in non-coding roles. This could be roles like "Business Operations Manager", "Customer Success Manager", or "Product Manager". Often this interviewer is someone that you'd collaborate with on a regular basis (think of them as an internal client or business partner). They're generally going to look at your problem-solving ability (case questions) and your mindset around working cross-functionally (ie., with people in roles outside your team). These are important to do well because your manager and the company needs to understand that people will enjoy working with you and it will be a productive experience for everyone. You probably won't get technical questions here (but it's possible), so focus on answering business problems as well as questions that focus on your ability to work with others. One possible question might be, "Tell me about a time you had to explain something technical to a non-technical person". For more examples, go ahead and search "Cross-functional interviews" online and see what you can dig up.

You may also meet with someone higher up, such as your boss's boss. This could be someone with a title anywhere from "Manager" to "Head of XYZ" to "Director" or "VP". These interviews may seem intimidating, but you shouldn't stress. The higher-up wants to know that you'll be a good fit for the team and have potential to grow and develop. They're also looking for any red flags that might pop up, such as "not being a team player". These are important and you should practice, but work on making a good impression and articulating your interest in the company and you should be good to go. As always, be prepared for business case questions and "Tell me about a time..." questions in case they come up.

The last type of interview we'll discuss is the culture interview. This is usually with someone who is at a similar level but on a different team, or it could be one of your teammates. That said, it could be anyone of any level, and it's often a wise choice to think of every interview as a culture interview.

Anyone in the interview roster may ask you questions about the company's mission, why you're interested, how you are to collaborate with, etc., because everyone wants to know that they're going to enjoy having you on the team. The good news is that the culture component of the interview process should be a place for you to shine. Write out the mission and think about how it resonates with you. Do your research and think about questions that might come up. Come up with a great answer for, "Why are you interested in this role?", and "Why do you want to work at ABC, Inc.?". Plenty of candidates will have the technical chops and problem-solving skills, and so will you- if it comes down to the culture fit, make sure you leave no stone unturned and have great answers.

These interviews go a lot further than questions about why you want to work at the company, or how you feel about their mission. Companies want to understand how you learn and how you approach your work. Here are some other questions you may be asked:

- Tell me about a time you failed

- Tell me about a time you had to give feedback to a teammate or coworker

- Tell me about a time when you taught yourself something new

In one sense, the culture interviews are easy because you're not being tested on a specific subject or being asked to whiteboard code, but in some ways they are more difficult. It's tough to prepare specific answers for all the possible questions, especially since you'll be asked to provide examples of specific situations that relate to the topic at hand. That said, you plan is simple: research questions ahead of time, go through the process of writing out questions and saying them out loud, and take your time when you're in the interview. When the interviewer asks you a question, it's OK to pause for a few moments and think of a good example. They understand that these questions aren't the easiest to answer, so feel free to take a little time to come up with something.

The key points to illustrate here are that you align with their culture, you're collaborative and good to work with, you have empathy for others, and you're reflective enough to learn from your mistakes. That's the kind of person companies want to hire, and if you put the work in you'll be able to stand out from the crowd.

The last thing we're going to cover in this section is what to do after the onsite interview. This is important, and unfortunately most candidates do great prep work before an interview, do a great job in the interview, but neglect to do a few simple, key things that can make a difference in their ultimate success.

First of all, the recruiter will often want to round up with you after all the interviews (in-person or over the phone). Their purpose is to check in, get your thoughts, and let you know they'll be following up. This is your opportunity to be nice and friendly, and express gratitude for all the work they've done. Thank them for organizing everything. Let the recruiter know you enjoyed chatting with everyone and had a great experience. You can also tee up the follow-up emails (more on that in a moment) by letting the recruiter know you'd love to send thank-you notes to the interviewers, and it would be great if he or she could send you the email addresses. Even though you're probably drained from bringing your A game all day, take time to be friendly with the recruiter. This may help you get considered for another opportunity in the future if the one you're on site for doesn't work out.

At the end of the day, send follow-up emails to the interviewers. Let them know you enjoyed chatting with them and learning about the team. Make each message slightly tailored to the person you're sending it to- if you had a great chat about optimizing user wait times for food delivery, go ahead and mention that.

Most candidates fall off here. They think they either did a great job in the interview or didn't, and they'll get the job or they won't. That is partially true. For most jobs in data fields, sending a follow-up note won't be the difference between getting the role or not.

So why send it? Because you want to keep the door open for future opportunities if the current one doesn't work out. You want to be just a little more memorable in some way. Sending a follow-up note can make a difference in you being considered for other roles in the future, so go ahead and thank them for their time.

Our final point applies only if you didn't get an offer. If this hasn't happened to you yet, it will. Even the best and brightest get rejected, so don't take it to heart. You'll have to do a postmortem and reflect on what you could have done better, but there is one action you can do right away: send another follow-up note, this time to just the hiring manager (and potentially their manager if you interviewed with them and had a good rapport). Yes, really.

    Here you're going to thank the hiring manager again, and let them know that although you're disappointed in the outcome, you enjoyed meeting and think it's "definitely the type of team you'd like to be a part of some day". Close the short email with, "Thanks again, and please don't hesitate to let me know if there are other opportunities in the future". Believe it or not, this tiny email can get you a job.

Thoughts from a Data Candidate

    "I rejected at my dream company (for my dream role) twice. The 2nd time, I sent a nice follow-up email to the hiring manager and let him know I enjoyed meeting his team and would love to hear about future opportunities. He got back to me a week later and offered me a role on his team- turns out he got approval from his boss to hire one more person, and he chose me. I still had to do great in the interview, but I do think the follow-up note made a difference."

    Most people are a bit nervous when it comes to follow-up notes, so don't worry. Just keep it short, friendly, and use the above guidelines. It might not get you a job right away, but developing these connections over time will help you become very successful. Remember this: whether or not you get offered a job, you absolutely always want to keep the door open for future opportunities. That means showing interviewers you're prepared, being friendly and amiable during the interview, and sending nice follow-up notes to show your appreciation. It just may land you an incredible opportunity in the future.

    That's about it for this section. We covered everything you need to know about the onsite interview, including how to prepare, how to knock it out of the park in the onsite itself, and how to set yourself up for success with thoughtful follow-ups. This section is meant to give you all the tools you need to be successful and get a great job offer, but keep in mind that there are a lot of variables outside of your control. You can't control who else is interviewing or how much experience they have. You can't change an interviewer's biases or preconceived notions about certain types of candidates. There are even some crazier things that affect your odds of success: what if the hiring manager had a tough conversation with their boss before the interview and is in an unforgiving mood? What if they had a bad lunch and are feeling ill?

    You can't prevent these things or even wrap your head around all the potential factors affecting the outcome- all you can do is work hard to prepare and do your best during and after the interview. If you don't get the job, don't worry or take it personally- just do a postmortem and figure out how you'll get better, then move on. If you do get the role, congratulations! Clearly the hard work paid off.

Know this: you will succeed over time as long as you work hard to prepare, reflect on failures, improve, and be flexible in your approach. That's the only recipe for success that is reliable and works consistently. Focus on what you can control and improve every single day.

Week 8

As you can tell by now, it's not likely that your progress follows the exact timeline laid out in this guide. Some candidates find themselves doing onsite interviews in the first two weeks (as opposed to the 5th week), while some candidates take much longer to gain traction. Your mileage may vary, so don't be too worried if you're not where you want to be yet.

This section is about reflection. All too often we get lost in the maze of trying to find a new job, and we don't stop to think about our progress at a higher level. You must learn to analyze yourself and identify things that are holding you back. This is a crucial step in improving, potentially even more so than working hard. Some people work hard all the time, but don't bother to figure out how to get better, and they burn themselves out in the process. You need to "sharpen the saw". A guide can't tell you what you're doing wrong, but it can help you ask the right questions and figure out for yourself how you can get better and ultimately reach your goal.

Let's get started. The basic theme here is that you want to look at your progress from a higher perspective: if you were evaluating and coaching yourself, what would you say? How would you think about your performance? This is not meant to be a negative exercise, and some candidates are far too harsh with themselves. You want to think about the good things you've done, so you can keep doing those things, and also identify what areas of the job search need some work. Pro tip: do this in writing so it will become ingrained in your mind. Here are some questions to consider:

How do you feel about your performance overall? Regardless of whether or not you got a job offer, how was your effort? It's important to be honest with yourself when you're thinking about the effort you put in to your job search. Is this something you worked on every day, or at least most days? Or did you take two weeks off in the middle of the process? Think about what grade you'd give yourself, from F at the lowest to A+ at the highest. Remember, it's better to be honest and give yourself a B than it is to bend the truth and give yourself an A+.

Now that you have your grade, why did you earn that grade? If it's an A-, why is it an A-? Use bullet points here, and make sure your talk about the positives in addition to the negatives (if you didn't do anything at all, you'd give yourself an F, and you probably wouldn't have made it as far as this section anyway). The positives could read something like, "I made the list of jobs and worked my way from the least-desirable to the most-desirable. I also did outreach every day, and when I had an interview I practiced by writing the questions out and saying them out loud".

The "room for improvement section" might read something like, "I didn't keep up the outreach every week, and when I did outreach I only did online job applications. I only applied for jobs through connections once or twice, but I know I could have done more. Also, when I had my first data challenge, I kind of just jumped in on the first question and didn't read and understand the entire prompt".

It's important to think about what you could have done better, even if you got a job offer. Here's a secret to success: even the people who are the best in the world at what they do think about how they can get better. They're always improving, even when they win the championship or execute an amazing business deal. How do you think Amazon became such a massively successful company? Jeff Bezos didn't say, "Oh, looks like we're the best online bookstore in the world. I guess we did it- time to retire". He kept asking how the company could get better. He thought about what they could do to radically improve their results.

That's what you're doing right now. You're doing an analysis of your performance looking for ways to improve. If you spent two months trying to get a job in data, but didn't get one- don't worry- you're not alone. Plenty of candidates take even longer than that. The fact that you tried to get a job but didn't get quite there should be totally motivating for you and you should be excited to learn and improve. Life is about growth. Finding a job is about learning (through resources like this chapter), making attempts, and learning from those attempts. As long as you're putting forth a good effort and learning from your results, you're succeeding.

Here are some more questions to ask yourself:

- Did I follow the instructions in the guide? Why or why not? In what ways could I have done better following the strategy?

- How was your level of outreach? Did you truly stretch yourself and reach out to connections, and connections of connections? Or did you say, "Oh, I shouldn't bother that person. We only worked together for a year and we're not exactly close friends". Think about how you could have created more opportunities for yourself, again, even if you ultimately received a job offer.

- What grade would you give yourself for interview preparation? Did you do your research? What about writing your answers down and practicing out loud? If you didn't, I can bet you didn't end up with the ideal outcome. What would you do differently next time?

- Was there anything in this strategy guide that proved to be incorrect? This is important. This is a fantastic section and a lot of hard work went into making it the best possible strategy for getting a job in data, but we can't pretend it's the gospel. Some parts may not work for everyone, and that's OK. Did you notice anything, and if so how would you change or modify your approach?

Make sure to write down the answers to these questions so they become ingrained in your mind. You want to really learn this stuff and improve next time- it's better to get a D- and learn from it than it is to get a B and not learn it (and most of the time a B isn't enough to get you your dream job).

Conclusion

Did you find this section useful? Did you follow the process outlined? If you did, you've either got a great job in data or are on your way to getting one. This has been a comprehensive look at what it takes to get your career started in this field, and hopefully it has been useful to you. Remember that this is not going to be your last job search, so let's review a few things:

First, a big part of the process is having the right plan in place. This chapter is your plan, and you can supplement it in any way you think would be helpful. Maybe you'd like to incorporate weekly coffee meetings with someone already in the world of data to get their feedback, or maybe you'd just like to take things a step further and have a friend "mock interview" you when you've got something lined up. Whether you do those things or just stick with the plan laid out in this chapter, the right strategy is going to help you find your way to success.

As we've mentioned before, there are a lot of uncontrollables when it comes to getting a job, particularly when it's a new field for you. Reflecting on your outcomes, learning, and coming up with a plan for implementation is absolutely within your control, and that's the secret of people who really succeed. You've got the plan. You're going to implement it. And, you're probably going to skin your knee here and there- you're going to mess up an interview, fail a data challenge, and probably not get the offer after an onsite. It's OK! Let this be your mantra: persevere intelligently. Don't just keep trying the same stuff over and over again. Reflect on your process as what you could have done better. See yourself from the third person, as if you were a totally different person analyzing your actions. What holes do you see? What could be done better? Don't forget to ask yourself positive questions too: what did you do right? What should you keep doing in the future? What were the success you did have, and what actions led you to those successes?

Asking yourself these questions and answering them is how you'll win over time, regardless of whether or not you're lucky, have the right degree, have the right background, or anything else. Constant improvement is how you win, and it's within your control. Persist and be positive.

Persevere intelligently. Try, learn, improve, and try again. You can do it.

www.ingramcontent.com/pod-product-compliance
Lightning Source LLC
Chambersburg PA
CBHW030957240526
45463CB00017B/2772